SCHOOL START STORYBOOKS: NIK THE NINJA

In this colourful illustrated storybook, part of the *School Start* series, children with language needs can explore the story of Nik the Ninja, and his disastrous night at Merryville Museum.

School Start Storybooks support language development in reception and Key Stage 1 aged children both in school and at home. Through beautifully illustrated stories, children are invited to explore language, ask questions and recall events in order to aid language development, listening and memory skills. Each book contains a colourful and engaging story designed to appeal to young children, and with language specifically chosen for children with language needs.

Key skills that these books support include:

- Comprehension
- Expression
- Vocabulary
- Memory
- Sequencing

Available either as a set or as individual books, the *School Start Storybooks* are a vital resource for professionals looking to support language development either with individual children, or groups of children. Each book also contains guidance and prompt questions to help the supporting adult use the book effectively, making it ideal for parents to support language development at home.

Catherine de la Bedoyere is a speech and language therapist with over 25 years' experience of working with children, including managing and delivering services in a variety of early years and school settings.

Liam de la Bedoyere is an illustrator and designer.

School Start

School Start is a series of practical resources to be used with children who need additional help in developing communication skills.

Pre-School Start: Targeted Intervention for Language Ages 3 and 4 (Reception – 1)
PB: 978-1-90930-175-7

School Start: Targeted Intervention for Language and Sound Awareness in Reception Class (2nd edition)
PB: 978-1-90939-158-0

School Start Year 1: Targeted Intervention for Language and Sound Awareness
PB: 978-1-13857-395-6

School Start Storybooks: Supporting Auditory Memory and Sequencing Skills in Key Stage 1 (Available as a set or as individual books)
PB: 978-1-138-34283-5

School Start Storybooks: Bozo the Clown
PB: 978-0-367-81017-7

School Start Storybooks: Nik the Ninja
PB: 978-0-367-40971-5

School Start Storybooks: Rusty the Robber
PB: 978-0-367-40972-2

School Start Storybooks

Nik the Ninja

Catherine de la Bedoyere

Liam de la Bedoyere

Routledge
Taylor & Francis Group

LONDON AND NEW YORK

First published 2020
by Routledge
2 Park Square, Milton Park, Abingdon, Oxon OX14 4RN

and by Routledge
52 Vanderbilt Avenue, New York, NY 10017

Routledge is an imprint of the Taylor & Francis Group, an informa business

British Library Cataloguing-in-Publication Data
A catalogue record for this book is available from the British Library

Library of Congress Cataloging-in-Publication Data
A catalog record for this book has been requested

ISBN: 978-0-367-40971-5 (pbk)
ISBN: 978-0-367-81022-1 (ebk)

Typeset in Calibri
by Apex CoVantage, LLC

School Start Storybooks support language development in children aged 5–7 at school and home. The books present stories that appeal to this age group, are adjusted for children with language needs and provide guides for the adult reader to help with:

Comprehension ☐

Expression ☐

Vocabulary ☐

Memory ☐

Sequencing ☐

'As a speech and language therapist, I find that sharing stories is an excellent way of introducing children with language needs to new language forms. By reading aloud picture books to children, we can explore new words, ask questions that prompt discussion and recall what has happened. However, it can be hard to find books that both interest this age group that are written in differentiated language. So I have created stories that are designed to be read aloud by an adult to a child, or group of children. I often talk to teaching assistants in schools about using spoken stories for language, as oppose to learning to read. They usually ask me how to ask questions, which words to talk about and how to demonstrate meaning; for this reason, I have included prompts and directions for adults throughout the text.' Catherine de la Bedoyere

Nik the Ninja also features in *School Start Year 1* Sound Awareness programme (2019) and it may be read alongside this group programme.

Instructions

Please read this story aloud to a child or group of children. Hold the book so that you can read the text and the children can see the illustration. Prompts to develop language are embedded in the text (see below). Do not deliver all the prompts and questions in the first reading; aim to introduce more on each re-reading of the story. Above all, please remember that sharing books is supposed to be a fun and interactive experience for children and adults alike.

Animated voice and expressions!

Children with limited language rely on tone of voice, gesture and facial expression to help them decode the meaning of words. We typically use this exaggeration with under fives, but children over five with limited language still benefit from your acting talents.

! will give you a prompt to add a little emphasis.

Miming and pointing

To help children understand the words in the story, mime the actions and point to the relevant illustrations. Children with limited language tend to be visual learners and will bootstrap their visual understanding to their verbal understanding if you provide this support.

Prompts to mime and point are printed in italics in the text.

Vocabulary

The text will introduce a variety of new words and word forms to children with plenty of repetition to aid learning. Children with difficulty learning and remembering new words need many more opportunities to hear the word in context than typically developing children. Reading the story many times gives multiple opportunities, but even better will be hearing the word in everyday use. Each time you read the book, focus on different words in the text and try to use the word in real life during that day, e.g. feelings such as happy and sad.

To focus on a word when reading the story:

* Say it clearly, stop and repeat it

* Encourage the children to ask you what it means

* Show what it means, e.g. point to Nik the Ninja

* Use gesture, e.g. say 'first' as you hold up one finger and 'next' as you hold up a second finger

* Suggest or compare a word or phrase with a similar meaning, e.g. cops/police, shake/tremble, nervous/scared

* Compare the word with the opposite meaning, e.g. heavy/light, happy/sad

* Compare different forms of the same word, e.g. catch/caught, leap/leapt, fly/flew, throw/threw

* In this book, emphasis is given to forms of dialogue (said, replied, yelled etc.) and ways of feeling (sad, shy, brave etc.); the many examples give you the opportunity to draw the children's attention to how words express meaning

Suggested vocabulary to teach is printed in **bold**.

Questions

Suggested questions are inserted into the story as a prompt for you.

Allow the children time to give you an answer. Children with limited language typically find the closed questions about something visual or concrete easier to answer, e.g. 'Do you get pocket money, Yes? No?' but may still need you to model alternative answers. Harder questions expect the child to relate the story to their own experience, e.g. 'Did you do something kind today?' Pause to give the children time to answer, but be ready to suggest or model an answer to scaffold their attempt to respond, e.g. 'Sometimes children are kind when they share their book in class', etc. Questions are used in the book to demonstrate how to understand and answer different question forms, as well as engaging children in the story as active listeners. They are not there to 'test' but to 'teach and engage'.

Questions are indicated in the text by colour and 'Q:'

Question prompt cards available in *School Start Year 1* may be used to aid understanding of the different question forms.

Memory: lists and information recall

To encourage active listening and develop short-term memory, play a question game with the children that will require them to recall what they have seen and discussed on that page.

At the end of the page, turn the book so the children cannot see the illustrations. Ask them the prompt questions so that they recall items as a group. Use the illustrations to confirm or prompt responses once the children have had a go at answering.

Memory: sequencing

Children learning and remembering verbal language are helped if they have a story structure that provides a frame; for instance what happened, first, next and last? This is why it can be so helpful to teach children a) sequencing terms ('first, next, last' or 'beginning, middle, end') and b) how to recall events in a sequence. As the child learns these foundation skills, it will become easier for them to understand the information given in the classroom. Stories are the natural place to develop sequencing skills. For this reason, the text frequently uses sequencing terms, such as 'finally'.

At the end of the story, there are prompt questions to recap the story sequence. Use the illustrations to confirm or prompt responses once the children have had a go at answering.

Sharing the story at home

Sit with your child so they can see the pictures.

Read the story to your child, pointing to the pictures to help them understand.

Use your acting skills (face and voice) to bring the words to life.

Next time you read the story, ask some of the questions. Pause to give your child time to answer; but if they struggle, tell them the answer.

Each time you read the story, ask more questions and stop to explain what a word (**in bold**) means.

Try and use new words at other times in the day to help your child become confident with the word.

Do not expect your child to read the written words; this is a listening activity, not a reading activity.

Stop if your child loses focus ☐

Sharing stories is fun ☐

Build on success ☐

Teach don't test ☐

Why this book may help your child at home

In class, children are expected to listen to the teacher, understand the information and follow instructions. To be successful at this, the children must be able to pay attention, listen, understand the words and grammar and finally remember what has been said in the right order. For some children, these skills are slower to develop than for others and typically these children will struggle in class. There are many ways to help such children but sharing stories can be one of the most enjoyable and simple activities to boost listening and language.

During infant school years, teaching places focus on children becoming readers. Reading will introduce children to more formal and complex language than they will hear in the playground and so it is an important part of child language development. Children who are having trouble with spoken language are likely to find learning to read and understand written words difficult. So for these children, it is important to continue to read stories aloud to them until they can read independently; this will make sure they are not missing out on the opportunity to extend their language experience.

Once upon a time, there was a **Ninja** called Nik. *(Point to the illustration.)*

Q: Do you know what a Ninja is?

Nik the Ninja is very clever; he is so quiet no one can hear him at all. He is the master of disguise. This means no one hears or sees him coming into the room.

Q: Can you be so quiet no one hears you come in the room? *(Close your eyes while the child tries to creep up on you without being heard.)*

Nik likes to steal things that belong to other people. So it is very useful to be quiet; it means Nik can creep up and take your things without you realising! But Nik doesn't want to steal your things; he wants to steal valuable loot, like gold and treasure.

Q: Now I wonder where Nik can find valuable loot to steal? Do you know where he can go?

This story is about the night that Nik broke into Merryville Museum and stole lots of loot.

Nik the Ninja opened a window in the roof and climbed down a long rope. He wore black clothes so he was invisible in the dark. On his face was a green mask. He wore green gloves and carried a staff.

Q: Why is Nik stealing from the museum at night-time?

Memory Questions:

Q: What colour was Nik's mask?

Q: How did Nik get into the museum?

Nik the Ninja planned exactly what he wanted to steal from the Merryville Museum displays. He darted and jumped **swiftly** about the museum, grabbing the loot and put it all into his rucksack. He had to be very **careful**; he did not want to set off the **burglar alarm**!

Q: Can you dart and jump swiftly like a Ninja? *(Set up a simple game by hiding objects around the room and challenge a child to find them, moving like a Ninja.)*

Memory Question:

Q: Why did Nik have to be careful?

Nik the Ninja's rucksack was so full of loot, it was very heavy. Nik swung the rucksack onto his back and climbed carefully up the rope to the window in the roof to make his escape. Up he climbed, **quietly, gently**... SHHHH!

The rucksack started to swing from side to side. DISASTER! Suddenly, the rucksack dropped all the way down to the museum floor.

And Nik was left **dangling** by his foot, all **tangled**, **twisted** and **tied up** in the rope!

What a surprise, because now Nik isn't quiet any more! 'HELP, HELP,' he cried. But there was no one to hear him because it was the middle of the night and the museum was **empty**.

Memory Question:

Q: Why is the museum empty?

The next morning the museum assistants came to work. They unlocked the museum front door. As they walked into the museum hall, they heard a very **tired**, **scared**, **small** cry of 'Help, help,' coming from up above!

Imagine their surprise when they looked up and saw Nik the Ninja dangling from a rope up in the air! Next, the **confused** museum assistants saw the rucksack on the floor and the loot spilling out everywhere.

'Oh no,' shouted a museum assistant. 'Nik the Ninja has been stealing from the museum.'

(Point out the museum assistants in the illustration.)

Memory Question:

Q: Who shouted, 'Nik the Ninja has been stealing from the museum'?

Now, we are going to help the museum assistants discover what Nik the Ninja has stolen.

Here is the Moon display. Can you see the **spaceship** and **Earth**?
Here is the **astronaut**.

Q: What do you think Nik stole from the Moon display?

The astronaut shouted out, 'Nik has stolen the big moon rock from the Moon display!'

Memory Questions:

Q: What did Nik steal from the Moon display?

Q: What do you call the person who goes into space?

Let's help the mermaid discover what Nik has stolen from the **aquarium** display. Here is the octopus and here is the **submarine**.

Q: What do you think Nik stole from the aquarium display?

The mermaid shouted out, 'Nik has stolen the gold from the red treasure chest in the aquarium display!'

Q: Do you know what lives in an aquarium? Sea creatures live in an aquarium.

Memory Questions:

Q: What sea creature lives in the aquarium display?

Q: What did Nik steal from the aquarium?

Here is the Viking assistant and the Viking display; here is the **ship**, **axe** and **lightning**. *(Point to the illustration.)*

Q: What do you think Nik stole from the Viking display?

Let's help the Viking find what Nik stole from the Viking display?

The Viking shouted out, 'Nik has stolen the Viking helmet from the Viking display!'

Memory Questions:

Q: Can you remember what Nik stole from the Viking display?

Q: What else was in the Viking display?

Can we help the **Egyptian** find what Nik stole from the Egyptian display?

Meet the Egyptian assistant at the Egyptian display; here is the **tomb**, **beetle**, **scorpion** and **mummy** wrapped in **bandages**. *(Point to the illustration.)*

Q: What do you think Nik stole from the Egyptian display?

The Egyptian shouted out, 'Nik has stolen the golden cat from the Egyptian display!'

Memory Questions:

Q: Can you remember what Nik stole from the Egyptian display?

Q: What else was in the Egyptian display?

GYPTIAN
DISPLAY

Here is the dinosaur display, where the assistant is dressed-up as a **caveman**; here is the **T.Rex**, **volcano** and **bones**. *(Point to the illustration.)*

Q: What do you think Nik stole from the dinosaur display?

The cave man shouted out, 'Nik has stolen the dinosaur egg with orange spots from the dinosaur display!'

Memory Questions:

Q: Can you remember what Nik stole from the dinosaur display?

Q: What else was in the dinosaur display?

Q: What was the assistant dressed up as?

DINOSAUR
DISPLAY

Last of all is the castle display. Can you see the **turrets, shields, drawbridge** and crown?
What is sleeping in front of the castle? *(Point to the illustration.)*

Here is the assistant. He is a knight wearing **armour**. It keeps him safe if he has a sword
fight.

Q: What did Nik take from the castle display?

The knight shouted out, 'Nik has stolen the **long, silver** sword from the castle display!'

Memory Questions:

Q: Can you remember what Nik stole from the castle display?

Q: What was sleeping in front of the castle?

Q: What does the soldier wear to stay safe in a sword fight?

CASTLE DISPLAY

The museum assistants were all very angry with Nik the Ninja for stealing from Merryville Museum.

'Call the cops, 999!' cried the mermaid!

Officer Gotcha drove **speedily** to the museum in her police van. She bravely climbed up the rope to rescue Nik.

'I've been after you for a long, long time and finally I've **caught** you,' said a delighted Officer Gotcha. 'It's off to jail with you,' as she got out her **handcuffs**. She tried to put them on Nik's **wrists**, but...OH NO!

Nik the Ninja is an expert at escaping. As soon as Nik's feet touched the ground Nik did a **double** backflip, a **triple** spin and in a flash, he had disappeared!

Q: Can you do a triple spin?

Memory Questions:

Q: What number did the mermaid call for the cops?

Q: What did Officer Gotcha want to put on Nik's wrists?

'Lock the doors,' shouted Officer Gotcha, 'so Nik can't get out of the museum. We've all got to look for him. Who can find him first?'

Officer Gotcha and all the museum assistants set off to look for Nik the Ninja in the museum displays.

Q: Where do you think Nik is hiding? Can you remember the museum displays where Nik might be hiding? *(Point to previous illustrations to prompt responses.)*

Finally, Officer Gotcha found Nik hiding in the Egyptian display **inside** the tomb. He had tried to disguise himself by wrapping himself up in the mummy's bandages. But clever Officer Gotcha saw him through his disguise.

'Here he is,' shouted Officer Gotcha. All the museum assistants clapped their hands **noisily** and cheered **loudly**.

'HURRAH!' they yelled.

'Well done, Officer Gotcha,' they called out.

Memory Question:

Q: Can you remember where Nik was hiding?

'Look at all the loot you have taken!' Officer Gotcha declared, showing him the rucksack full of loot.

But Nik didn't look sorry. He didn't look sad. He looked very, very cross that Officer Gotcha had **found** him.

'Are you going to say sorry to the museum assistants?' asked Officer Gotcha.

'NO WAY!' shouted Nik **firmly**. 'NEVER!'

Q: Do you think Nik is naughty or nice?

Memory Question:

Q: What loot did Nik steal?

Nik tried to escape AGAIN. But when he tried to run ... OH NO! He was all tangled in the bandages and tied up to the tomb. Look, the scorpion is making sure he doesn't escape.

'Right,' said Officer Gotcha. 'I've got you now and I'm going to teach you a lesson.'

'You can't escape because you have got yourself all tangled up. You can stay there and think about how naughty it is to steal. I will only untangle you when you feel sorry for stealing.'

Look, here he is in the Egyptian display with Officer Gotcha. Now everyone can come and see naughty Nik the Ninja **stuck** in the museum display **until** he says sorry!

The End.

Q: Do you think Nik said sorry?

Q: Or do you think he is still stuck there in the Egyptian display?